EXECUTIVE SUMMARY

Developing Literacy in Second-Language Learners: Report of the National Literacy Panel on Language-Minority Children and Youth

Edited by

Diane August
Principal Investigator

Timothy Shanahan
Panel Chair

 LAWRENCE ERLBAUM ASSOCIATES, PUBLISHERS
2006 Mahwah, New Jersey   London

Copyright © 2006 by Lawrence Erlbaum Associates, Inc.
All rights reserved. No part of this book may be reproduced in any form, by photostat, microform, retrieval system, or any other means, without prior written permission of the publisher.

Lawrence Erlbaum Associates, Inc., Publishers
10 Industrial Avenue
Mahwah, New Jersey 07430
www.erlbaum.com

Cover design by Tomai Maridou

CIP information for this book can be obtained by contacting the Library of Congress

ISBN 0-8058-6078-9 (pbk. : alk. paper)

Books published by Lawrence Erlbaum Associates are printed on acid-free paper, and their bindings are chosen for strength and durability.

Printed in the United States of America
10 9 8 7 6 5 4 3 2 1

Contents

The contents of the entire volume, *Developing Literacy in Second-Language Learners: Report of the National Literacy Panel on Language-Minority Children and Youth,* from which this Executive Summary is adapted, are listed below.

Foreword

Preface

Introduction to the Volume

1 **Introduction and Methodology**
Diane August and Timothy Shanahan

2 **Demographic Overview**
Diane August

PART I: Development of Literacy in Second-Language Learners

3 **Synthesis: Development of Literacy in Language-Minority Students**
Nonie Lesaux and Esther Geva

4 **Development of Literacy**
Nonie Lesaux with Keiko Koda, Linda S. Siegel, and Timothy Shanahan

5 **Second-Language Oral Proficiency and Second-Language Literacy**
Esther Geva

Part I References

PART II: Cross-Linguistic Relationships in Second-Language Learners

6 Synthesis: Cross-Linguistic Relationships
Fred Genesee, Esther Geva, Cheryl Dressler, and Michael L. Kamil

7 Cross-Linguistic Relationships in Working Memory, Phonological Processes, and Oral Language
Fred Genesee and Esther Geva

8 First-Language Oral Proficiency and Second-Language Literacy
Esther Geva and Fred Genesee

9 First-and Second-Language Literacy
Cheryl Dressler with Michael L. Kamil

Part II References

PART III: Sociocultural Contexts and Literacy Development

10 Synthesis: Sociocultural Contexts and Literacy Development
Claude Goldenberg, Robert S. Rueda, and Diane August

11 Social and Cultural Influences on the Literacy Attainment of Language-Minority Children and Youth
Claude Goldenberg, Robert S. Rueda, and Diane August

12 The Social and Cultural Context in which Children Acquire Literacy
Robert S. Rueda, Diane August, and Claude Goldenberg

Part III References

PART IV: Educating Language-Minority Students: Instructional Approaches and Professional Development

13 Synthesis: Instruction and Professional Development
Diane August and Timothy Shanahan

14 Language of Instruction
David J. Francis, Nonie Lesaux, and Diane August

15 Effective Literacy Teaching for English-Language Learners
Timothy Shanahan and Isabel L. Beck

16 Qualitative Studies of Classroom and School Practices
Diane August with Frederick Erickson

17 Literacy Instruction for Language-Minority Children in Special Education Settings
Diane August with Linda S. Siegel

CONTENTS

18 Teacher Beliefs and Professional Development
Diane August and Margarita Calderón

Part IV References

PART V: Student Assessment

19 Synthesis: Language and Literacy Assessment
Georgia Earnest García, Gail McKoon, and Diane August

20 Language and Literacy Assessment of Language-Minority Students
Georgia Earnest García and Gail McKoon

Part V References

21 Cross-Cutting Themes and Future Research Directions
Catherine Snow

Biographical Sketches

EXECUTIVE SUMMARY

Diane August
Principal Investigator

Timothy Shanahan
Panel Chair

Teaching language-minority students to read and write well in English is an urgent challenge in the nation's K–12 schools. Literacy in English is essential to achievement in every academic subject—and to educational and economic opportunities beyond schooling.

Compounding this challenge are increasing numbers and diversity of language-minority students. These indicators illuminate the challenge:

- A large and growing number of students come from homes where English is not the primary language. In 1979, there were 6 million language-minority students; by 1999, this number had more than doubled to 14 million students.
- Some language-minority students are not faring well in U.S. schools. For the 41 states reporting, only 18.7% of English-language learners scored above the state-established norm for reading comprehension (Kindler, 2002).
- Whereas 10% of students who spoke English at home failed to complete high school, the percentage was three times as high (31%) for language-minority students who spoke English and five times as high (51%) for language-minority students who spoke English with difficulty (National Center for Education Statistics, 2004).

Language-minority students who cannot read and write proficiently in English cannot participate fully in American schools, workplaces, or society. They face limited job opportunities and earning power. Nor are the consequences of low literacy attainment in English limited to individual impoverishment. U.S. economic competitiveness depends on workforce quality. Inadequate reading and writing proficiency in English relegates rapidly increasing language-minority populations to the sidelines, limiting the nation's potential for economic competitiveness, innovation, productivity growth, and quality of life.

The importance of this challenge led the U.S. Department of Education's Institute of Education Sciences to create the National Literacy Panel on Language-Minority Children and Youth.

Charge to the Panel

The formal charge to the panel was to identify, assess, and synthesize research on the education of language-minority children and youth with regard to literacy attainment and to produce a comprehensive report on this literature.

Background on the Panel

Developing Literacy in Second-Language Learners is the culmination of a 4-year process that began in the spring of 2002, when the Institute of Education Sciences staff selected a panel of 13 experts in second-language development, cognitive development, curriculum and instruction, assessment, and methodology to review the quantitative and qualitative research on the development of literacy in language-minority students.

This national panel identified five research topics to investigate:

- Development of literacy.
- Cross-linguistic relationships.
- Sociocultural contexts and literacy development.
- Instruction and professional development.
- Student assessment.

The panel formulated a series of research questions to guide the investigation of each topic. To address these questions, the panel formed five subcommittees, one devoted to each topic. The panel held five panel meetings and several subcommittee meetings, collaborating to outline, discuss, and review the substantive issues and relevant literature. The panel also held several open meetings to gain public advice and input from educators, community members, and researchers.

The report has undergone two rounds of external review by anonymous reviewers selected by the U.S. Department of Education, and substantial revisions in response to these reviews.

Funding for the project was provided to SRI International and the Center for Applied Linguistics by the Institute of Education Sciences and the Office of English Language Acquisition. Funding also was provided by the National Institute of Child Health and Human Development through funds transferred to the U.S. Department of Education.

The Panel's Approach to the Research

The panel established strict criteria for identifying appropriate, relevant research of sufficient quality to allow the research questions to be answered soundly. Two of these criteria merit discussion here:

- First, to ensure a rigorous research review, the panel required evidence from particular types of studies to answer particular types of questions. The issue here is appropriateness. For example, when the panel tried to determine whether particular approaches to instruction conferred advantages to language-minority students, the panel required experimental or quasi-experimental data. Other kinds of studies were used to answer other questions that did not require this kind of causal linkage.
- Second, to ensure the most relevance to policies and practices in U.S. schools, the panel focused on studies of second-language acquisition in which the target second language is English and the students are language-minority. However, the panel included studies of other target languages as well, if these studies could shed light on the challenges that students face in U.S. schools.

A final important point—and, perhaps, a key finding in its own right—is that the research on acquiring literacy in a second language remains limited. While the key findings summarized herein are supported by research evidence, the research on some topics is scant.

Developing Literacy in Second-Language Learners will be of particular value to researchers interested in the development of literacy in language-minority students. Sections will be relevant to researchers studying literacy more generally, as well as to practitioners concerned about improving the education of language-minority students.

Major Findings of the Panel

Instruction that provides substantial coverage in the key components of reading—identified by the National Reading Panel (NICHD, 2000) as phonemic awareness, phonics, fluency, vocabulary, and text comprehension—has clear benefits for language-minority students.

Focusing on these key components of reading has a positive influence on the literacy development of language-minority students, just as it does for native English speakers. Likewise, writing instruction has clear benefits for language-minority students, as it does for native English speakers.

Enhanced teaching of the key components of English literacy provides a clear advantage to English-language learners. In addition more complex, innovative programs typically taught several of these components simultaneously—and these efforts were usually successful in improving literacy for language-minority students. However, while approaches that are similar to those used with native-language populations are effective, the research suggests that adjustments to these approaches are needed to have maximum benefit with language-minority students. For example, young Spanish-speaking students learning to read in English might make the best progress when given more work with particular phonemes and combinations of phonemes in English that do not exist in their home language.

Becoming literate in a second language depends on the quality of teaching, which is a function of the content coverage, intensity or thoroughness of instruction, methods used to support the special language needs of second-language learners and to build on their strengths, how well learning is monitored, and teacher preparation. Teachers can learn how to deliver innovative instruction with effective professional development. Teachers found professional development to be most helpful when it provided opportunities for hands-on practice with teaching techniques readily applicable in their classrooms, in-class demonstrations with their own or a colleague's students, or personalized coaching, a finding that is consistent with previous research. Collaboration with special education teachers and resource specialists also improves the quality of instruction. In all the studies reviewed, outside collaborators with expertise (university researchers) assisted in professional development, suggesting that outside "change agents" can help teachers improve their classroom practices.

Instruction in the key components of reading is necessary—but not sufficient—for teaching language-minority students to read and write proficiently in English. Oral proficiency in English is critical as well—but student performance suggests that it is often overlooked in instruction.

An important finding that emerges from the research is that word-level skills in literacy—such as decoding, word recognition and spelling—are often taught well enough to allow language-minority students to attain levels of performance equal to those of native English speakers. However, this is not the case for text-level skills—reading comprehension and writing. Language-minority students rarely approach the same levels of proficiency in text-level skills achieved by native English speakers.

The research suggests that the reason for the disparity between word- and text-level skills among language-minority students is oral English proficiency. Oral proficiency in English is not a strong predictor of English word-level skills, although it is likely to correlate to some extent with the underlying cognitive skills (letter-sound awareness, rapid naming of words, and phonological memory) that do predict word identification skills in both language-minority students and native English speakers.

By contrast, well-developed oral proficiency in English *is* associated with English reading comprehension and writing skills for these students. Specifically, English vocabulary knowledge, listening comprehension, syntactic skills, and the ability to handle metalinguistic aspects of language, such as providing definitions of words, are linked to English reading and writing proficiency.

These findings help explain why many language-minority students can keep pace with their native English-speaking peers when the instructional focus is on word-level skills, but lag behind when the instructional focus turns to reading comprehension and writing.

Instructional approaches found to be successful with native English speakers do not have as positive a learning impact on language-minority students. It is not enough to teach language-minority students reading skills alone. Extensive oral English development must be incorporated into successful literacy instruction. The most promising instructional practices for language-minority students bear out this point: Literacy programs that provide instructional support of oral language development in English, aligned with high-quality literacy instruction are the most successful.

The patterns of learning across these studies suggest that the basic sequencing of teaching is likely to be the same for language-minority students and native English speakers—with greater attention to word-level skills early in the process and more direct and ambitious attention to reading comprehension later on. However, vocabulary and background knowledge, should be targeted intensively throughout the

EXECUTIVE SUMMARY

entire sequence. The need to develop stronger English-language proficiency to become literate in English argues for an early, ongoing, and intensive effort to develop this oral proficiency.

Oral proficiency and literacy in the first language can be used to facilitate literacy development in English.

Language-minority students are not blank slates. They enter classrooms with varying degrees of oral proficiency and literacy in their first language. There is clear evidence that tapping into first-language literacy can confer advantages to English-language learners. For example, there is evidence that language-minority students are able to take advantage of higher order vocabulary skills in the first language, such as the ability to provide formal definitions and interpret metaphors, when speaking a second language. Studies also indicate that students are able to take advantage of cognate relationships between their first language and English to understand English words, an important precursor to comprehension. There is limited evidence as well that cognate knowledge is associated with the development of reading comprehension in English. Cognates are words that have similar spellings and meanings in two languages, such as "continue" in English and "continuar" in Spanish.

First-language oral proficiency also influences developmental patterns in second-language speech discrimination, speech production, intraword segmentation, and vocabulary, which reflect the patterns of the first language—at least until students become more proficient in English.

There is ample evidence as well that first-language literacy is related in other important ways to literacy development in English, including word and pseudoword reading, reading comprehension, reading strategies, spelling, and writing. Language-minority students who are literate in their first language are likely to be advantaged in the acquisition of English literacy. It is important to take into consideration the transferability of some literacy skills, then, when planning and providing second-language literacy instruction to students who are literate in their first language.

Moreover, the research indicates that instructional programs work when they provide opportunities for students to develop proficiency in their first language. Studies that compare bilingual instruction with English-only instruction demonstrate that language-minority students instructed in their native language as well as in English perform better, on average, on measures of English reading proficiency than language-minority students instructed only in English. This is the case at both the elementary and secondary levels.

Individual differences contribute significantly to English literacy development.

Research shows that the development of English literacy entails cumulative, hierarchical processes for all language-minority students. Certain components of literacy cannot fully develop until students acquire other, precursor skills. For students to develop efficient word recognition skills, for example, they must first have good decoding and orthographic, or spelling, skills. Without fast and accurate word recognition skills, they cannot achieve satisfactory levels of reading comprehension.

However, English literacy development is a dynamic process and is influenced by individual differences in general language proficiency, age, English oral proficiency, cognitive abilities, previous learning, and the similarities and differences between the first language and English. For example, adolescent language-minority students schooled only in their first language may have well-developed phonological skills in both languages, but a similar level of development would not be as likely for 6-year-olds, who are cognitively less advanced in this regard. Similarly, older language-minority students are more likely than primary-level learners to notice cognates common to Spanish and English.

Reading difficulties among language-minority students may be more a function of individual differences than of language-minority status. Similar proportions of language-minority students and monolingual English speakers are classified as poor readers. In fact, with the exception of English oral-language skills, the profiles of poor readers in the two groups are very similar. Both groups demonstrate difficulties with phonological awareness and working memory. These findings suggest that underlying processing deficits, as opposed to language-minority status, are the primary issue for students experiencing word-level difficulties.

Interestingly, in studies of middle school students with reading difficulties, the language-minority students had better scores on phonological measures than their native English-speaking peers. This finding should be further investigated, since it differs from the findings on younger learners.

Finally, researchers have questioned the view that learning abilities and disabilities are inherent, rather than the result of the situational context. In fact, studies reveal that, given proper instruction, some language-minority students classified as learning disabled can achieve grade-level norms.

Furthermore, there is evidence of promising practices for language-minority students in special education settings. Behavioral approaches to developing sight word reading and vocabulary, cognitive or learning strategy approaches, and holistic, interactive approaches that encourage thoughtful discussion of ideas—all approaches grounded in very different theoretical models—are some examples. However, the small sample sizes and lack of controls in studies of these approaches demand more research to explore their effectiveness.

Most assessments do a poor job of gauging individual strengths and weaknesses.

The research on the development of English literacy strongly suggests that adequate assessments are essential for gauging the individual strengths and weaknesses of language-minority students, making placement decisions, and tailoring instruction to meet student needs. Unfortunately, existing assessments are inadequate to the need in most respects. For example, most measures do not predict how well language-minority students will perform over time on reading or content-area assessments in English.

For predictive purposes, several researchers found that letter naming and tests of phonological awareness in English were good predictors of performance in English reading. Because the researchers did not control for students' oral English proficiency or examine their first-language literacy performance on the same measures, however, the findings must be qualified. Although several researchers used criterion measures to identify low performers or students with reading difficulties, findings that some low-performing students substantially improved their reading performance with instruction suggest that additional longitudinal studies are needed to test the predictors against students' actual reading performance.

For placement purposes, there is limited evidence about the effectiveness of teacher judgment in identifying language-minority students who need intensive reading instruction or who might be in danger of dropping out of school. The find-

EXECUTIVE SUMMARY

7

ings suggest, however, that teacher judgment might be more reliable when teachers can respond thoughtfully to specific criteria rather than express their opinions spontaneously. Because teacher judgment and assessment play a significant role in the education of language-minority students, additional research needs to explore this assessment tool further.

Almost all of the researchers who examined the eligibility of language-minority students for special education, language disorders, or learning disabilities services recommend assessing students in both their first language and English. Very little research has focused on identifying older language-minority students with learning disabilities—another important issue for future study.

There is surprisingly little evidence for the impact of sociocultural variables on literacy achievement or development. However, home language experiences can have a positive impact on literacy achievement.

The panel investigated the effects of six sociocultural factors on literacy achievement and development: immigration status; discourse/interactional characteristics; other sociocultural factors; parents and family influences; district, state, and federal policies; and language status or prestige. With some exceptions, there is little evidence for gauging the impact of most of these factors. However, this does not mean that these factors have no impact. Rather, this finding reflects a shortcoming in the research, with studies tending to be descriptive rather than documenting empirical links between sociocultural factors and student outcomes, broadly defined.

The research does suggest that bridging home–school differences in interaction patterns or styles can enhance students' engagement, motivation, and participation in classroom instruction. This finding is not trivial, but it is still important to determine if bridging home–school differences consequently improves literacy achievement or development.

The research also suggests that students perform better when they read or use material that is in the language they know better. Culturally meaningful or familiar reading material also appears to facilitate comprehension, but this is a relatively weak predictor of reading comprehension compared to the language of the material and students' proficiency in that language.

Overall, student performance in literacy is more likely to be the result of home (and school) language and literacy learning opportunities. The research supports three findings about the role of home language for English-language learners' literacy achievement in English:

- First, language-minority parents express willingness—and often have the ability- -to help their children succeed academically. For various reasons, however, schools underestimate and underutilize parents' interest, motivation, and potential contributions.
- Second, more home literacy experiences and opportunities are associated with superior literacy outcomes, although findings in this regard are inconsistent and precise conclusions are difficult to find. Measures of parent and family literacy often predict children's literacy attainment, but two studies found that parents' reading behavior is unrelated to children's literacy outcomes. Features of family life, such as domestic workload and religious activities, appear to influence the value children place on reading and their concepts of themselves as readers. Parent education is associated with children's literacy outcomes as well.

- Third, the relationship between home language use and literacy achievement in English is unclear. In general, home experiences with the first and second languages are positively (but modestly) correlated with literacy achievement in the first and second languages, but negatively (and also modestly) correlated with literacy achievement in the second language. Four studies countered this generalization, however. As a result, there is insufficient evidence to make policy and practice recommendations about home language use.

Conclusion

The National Literacy Panel on Language-Minority Children and Youth systematically and rigorously examined the research on acquiring literacy in a second language. Through this process, the panel learned what is known—and what is not yet known—about the complex process of learning to read and write in a second language.

Policymakers and educators can use the panel's findings to benchmark their own practices and infuse research-based instruction into literacy programs for language-minority students. Researchers can enrich this knowledge base by focusing on the specific gaps in our knowledge, which in the future will enable U.S. schools to better educate English-language learners in English literacy.

References

Kindler, A. L. (2002). *Survey of the states' limited English proficient students and available educational programs and services: 2000–2001 summary report*. Washington, DC: National Clearinghouse for English Language Acquisition.

National Center for Education Statistics. (2004). *The condition of education, 2004*. Retrieved July 16, 2004, from http://nces.ed.gov/programs/coe

National Institute of Child Health and Human Development (NICHD). (2000). *Report of the National Reading Panel. Teaching children to read: An evidence-based assessment of the scientific research literature on reading and its implications for reading instruction* (NIH Publication No. 00-4769). Washington, DC: U.S. Department of Health and Human Services.

The *Executive Summary* is made available with permission from Lawrence Erlbaum Associates, Inc., publishers of D. August & T. Shanahan, Eds. (in press). *Developing Literacy in Second-Language Learners: A Report of the National Literacy Panel on Language-Minority Children and Youth*_(0-8058-6077-0, Mahwah, NJ: Lawrence Erlbaum Associates, Inc.).

For ordering information see http://www.erlbaum.com/august.

EXECUTIVE SUMMARY

NATIONAL LITERACY PANEL ON LANGUAGE-MINORITY CHILDREN AND YOUTH

Members of the National Literacy Panel

Diane August, Principal Investigator
Center for Applied Linguistics

Isabel Beck
University of Pittsburgh

Margarita Calderón
Johns Hopkins University

David J. Francis
University of Houston

Georgia Earnest García
University of Illinois, Urbana-Champaign

Esther Geva
University of Toronto

Fred Genesee
McGill University

Timothy Shanahan, Chair
University of Illinois, Chicago

Claude Goldenberg
California State University, Long Beach

Michael Kamil
Stanford University

Keiko Koda
Carnegie Mellon University

Gail McKoon
Ohio State University

Robert S. Rueda
University of Southern California

Linda Siegel
University of British Columbia

Panel Methodologists

Frederick Erickson
University of California, Los Angeles

David Francis
University of Houston

Senior Advisors to the Panel

Donna Christian
Center for Applied Linguistics

Catherine Snow
Harvard University

Senior Research Associates

Cheryl Dressler
Center for Applied Linguistics

Nonie Lesaux
Harvard University